MAR 1 8 2004

W9-BYF-412

The Mess

The Mess

Written by Patricia Jensen

Illustrated by Anthony Lewis

My First READER

children's press®

A Division of Scholastic Inc.
New York Toronto London Auckland Sydney
Mexico City New Delhi Hong Kong
Danbury, Connecticut

Library of Congress Cataloging-in-Publication Data

Jensen, Patricia.
  The mess / written by Patricia Jensen ; illustrated by Anthony
Lewis.– 1st American ed.
      p. cm. – (My first reader)
Summary: Easy-to-read rhyming tale of a boy who reflects on the
pleasures his friends are enjoying while he is stuck at home because he
made a mess.
  ISBN 0-516-22932-X (lib. bdg.)   0-516-24634-8 (pbk.)
  [1. Orderliness–Fiction. 2. Play–Fiction. 3. Stories in rhyme.] I.
Lewis, Anthony, 1966- ill. II. Title. III. Series.
  PZ8.3.J424Me 2003
  [E]–dc21
                                    2003003692

Text © 1990 Nancy Hall, Inc.
Illustrations © 2003 Anthony Lewis
Published in 2003 by Children's Press
A Division of Scholastic Inc.

1 2 3 4 5 6 7 8 9 10 R 12 11 10 09 08 07 06 05 04 03

Note to Parents and Teachers

Once a reader can recognize and identify the 20 words
used to tell this story, he or she will be able to read successfully
the entire book. These 20 words are repeated throughout the story,
so that young readers will be able to easily recognize
the words and understand their meaning.

The 20 words used in this book are:

a	go	my	the
friends	mess	slide	down
made	run	cleaned	I've
play	cannot	I	outside
can	hide	now	today

I cannot go outside today.

I made a mess.

I cannot play.

My friends can run.

My friends can hide.

My friends can go
slide down the slide.

17

I cannot run.

I cannot hide.

I cannot go slide
down the slide.

I've cleaned the mess!

Now I can play!

Now I can go outside today!

ABOUT THE AUTHOR

Patricia Jensen lives in New Jersey, has five children, three dogs, and is a stay-at-home mom.

ABOUT THE ILLUSTRATOR

Since graduating with First Class Honours from the Liverpool School of Art in 1989, **Anthony Lewis** has illustrated more than 200 children's books as well as magazine articles, advertisements, theater posters, and corporate brochures. In his free time, he enjoys the theater and traveling. He lives in Cheshire, England, with his wife, Kathryn, their young daughter, and two cats.